W9-CNA-244

The U.S. Constitution

by Norman Pearl ~ illustrated by Matthew Skeens

PICTURE WINDOW BOOKS
Minneapolis, Minnesota

Special thanks to our advisers for their expertise:

Kevin Byrne, Ph.D., Professor of History
Gustavus Adolphus College

Susan Kesselring, M.A., Literacy Educator
Rosemount–Apple Valley–Eagan (Minnesota) School District

❧

Editor: Jill Kalz
Designer: Nathan Gassman
Page Production: Tracy Kaehler and Ellen Schofield
Creative Director: Keith Griffin
Editorial Director: Carol Jones
The illustrations in this book were created digitally.

Picture Window Books
5115 Excelsior Boulevard, Suite 232
Minneapolis, MN 55416
877-845-8392
www.picturewindowbooks.com

Printed in the United States of America.

Library of Congress Cataloging-in-Publication Data
Pearl, Norman.
The U.S. Constitution / by Norman Pearl ; illustrated by Matthew Skeens.
p. cm. — (American symbols)
Includes bibliographical references and index.
ISBN-13: 978-1-4048-2643-4 (hardcover)
ISBN-10: 1-4048-2643-2 (hardcover)
ISBN-13: 978-1-4048-2646-5 (paperback)
ISBN-10: 1-4048-2646-7 (paperback)
1. Constitutional law—United States—Juvenile literature. 2. Constitutional history—
United States—Juvenile literature. I. Skeens, Matthew. II. Title. III. American
symbols (Picture Window Books)
KF4550.Z9P42 2007
342.7302—dc22   2006003377

Table of Contents

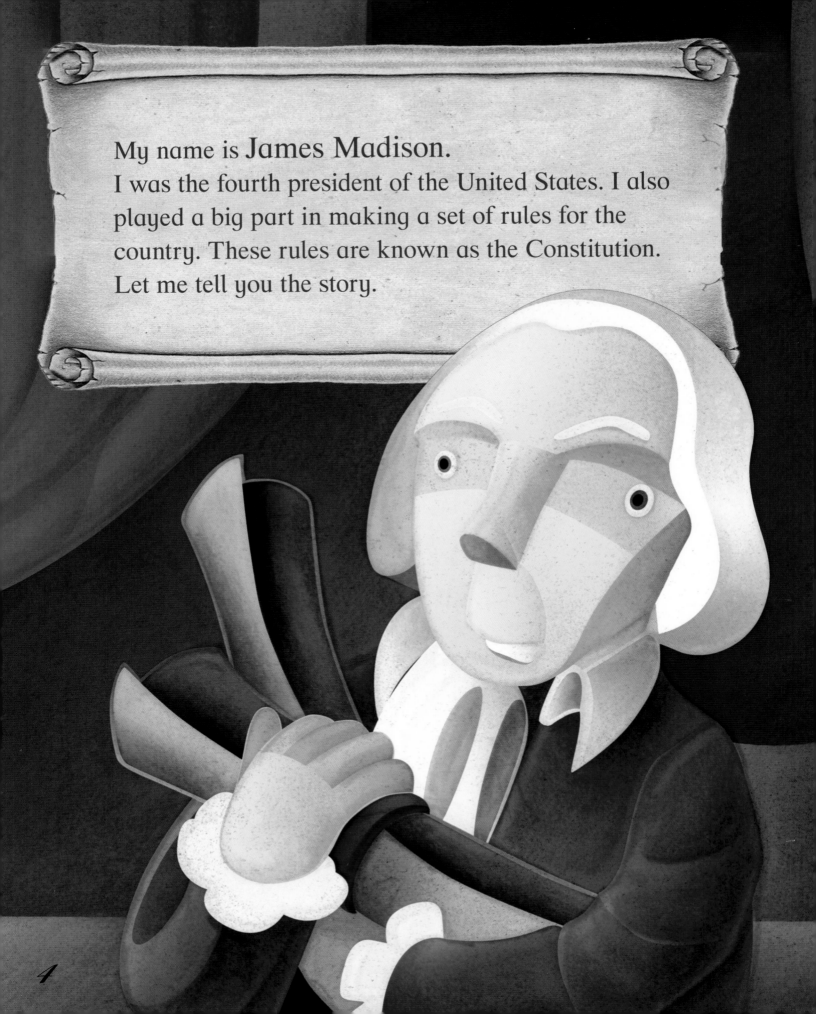

My name is James Madison.
I was the fourth president of the United States. I also played a big part in making a set of rules for the country. These rules are known as the Constitution. Let me tell you the story.

What Is the U.S. Constitution?

The Constitution of the United States is the plan for how the government works. It says how much power the branches, or parts, of the government can have. It tells them how to make laws and how to make sure all Americans follow them. The Constitution is a symbol of democracy.

The Constitution is the highest law in the United States. It is more important than any city or state law.

The First Rules of the United States

After winning the Revolutionary War in 1783, the United States was a new country. Like any country, it needed rules. Its first set of rules was called the Articles of Confederation. These rules joined together the 13 states.

It was a start, but the country needed more. The United States needed a better form of government.

Who Wrote the Constitution?

In May 1787, delegates from most of the 13 states met in Philadelphia, Pennsylvania. Their job was to write the Constitution, a new set of rules for the country's government.

8

The meeting was called the Constitutional Convention. The 55 delegates at the meeting later became known as the Framers of the Constitution.

Rhode Island was the only state that did not send any delegates to the Constitutional Convention.

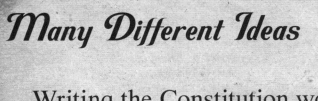

Many Different Ideas

Writing the Constitution was not easy. Many people had different ideas about what it should say. Some men wanted a strong national government. Others did not. There was a lot of arguing.

Finally, on September 17, 1787, the arguing stopped, and the delegates signed the Constitution. Then the states had to agree to follow it. The last one did so in 1790.

James Madison was a delegate from Virginia. He helped the other delegates at the Constitutional Convention work through their differences. Madison was both smart and fair. He is known today as the Father of the Constitution.

The Parts of the Constitution

The Constitution has three main parts: the preamble, the articles, and the amendments.

1. PREAMBLE

The preamble is the beginning of the Constitution. The preamble tells Americans why they need a government and a Constitution.

We the People of the United States, in Order to form a more perfect Union, establish Justice, insure domestic Tranquility, provide for the common defense, promote the general Welfare, and secure the Blessings of Liberty to ourselves and our Posterity, do ordain and establish this Constitution for the United States of America.

13

2. ARTICLES

The seven articles of the Constitution explain the branches of the U.S. government. They tell what those branches can and cannot do. In the United States, the people run the government. Americans have the right to vote. When they vote, Americans choose the people who will work for them in the government.

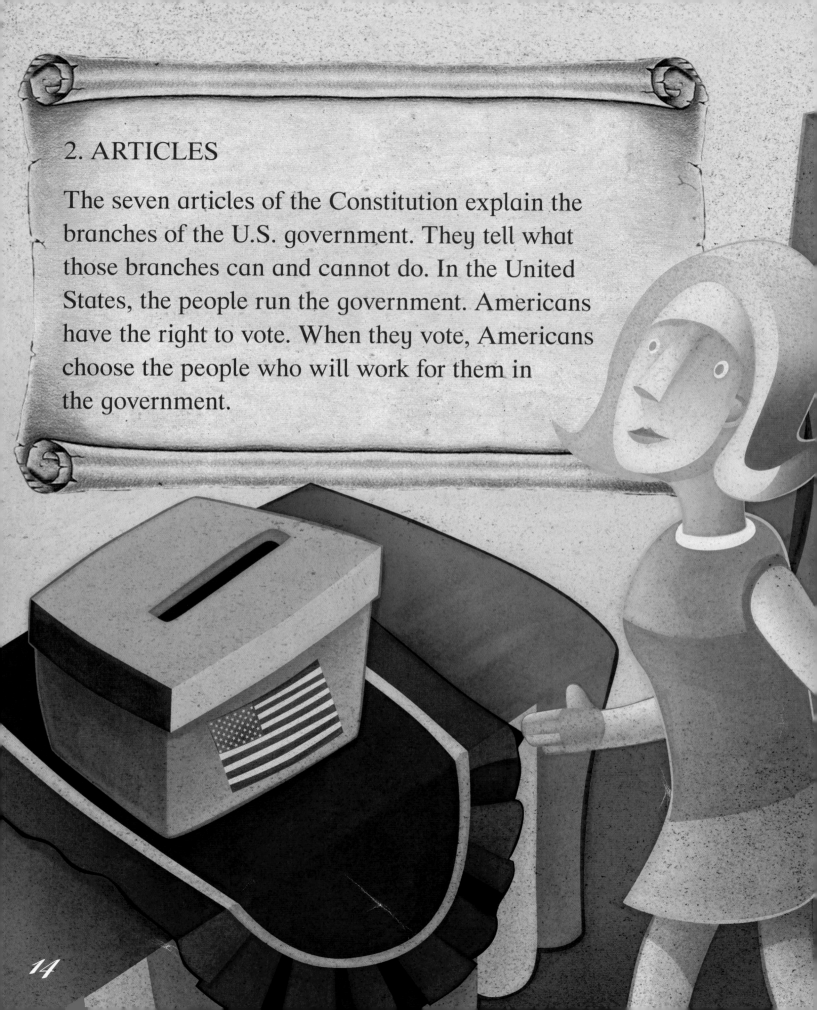

The articles allow people in government to keep all Americans safe. They say that the government can build an army and a navy to guard the country.

The articles divide the U.S. government into three branches. Each branch has different powers. No one branch can become stronger than the others. This is called a "balance of power." Every branch is equal.

The Executive Branch

This branch is made up of the president, the vice president, and the people who help them do their jobs. It is headquartered in the White House.

The Judicial Branch

This branch is the court system. Judges see that laws are carried out in the right way. The Judicial Branch is headquartered in the Supreme Court, the highest court in the United States.

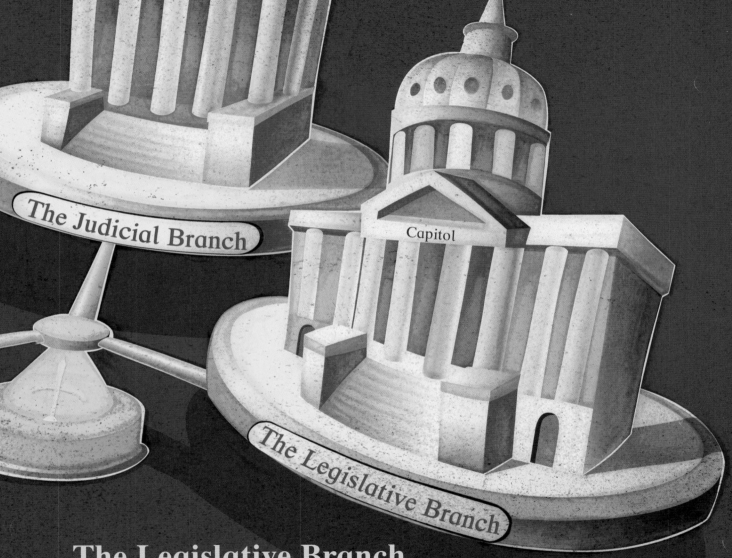

The Legislative Branch

This branch is made up of the Congress, which is divided into two parts: the House of Representatives and the Senate. Congress makes the nation's laws. It is headquartered in the Capitol.

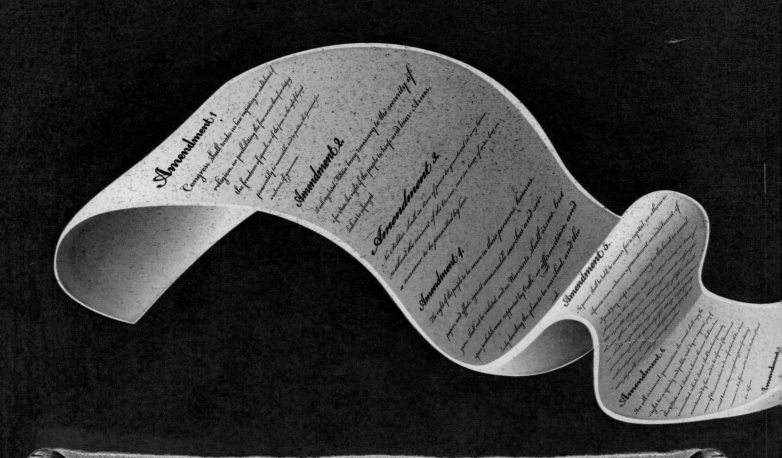

3. AMENDMENTS

The amendments were not part of the original Constitution. They were added later. They give Americans many rights. For example, the amendments say that Americans cannot be made slaves. They can belong to any religion they want. All Americans age 18 and older can vote. Since it was signed in 1787, the Constitution has been amended, or added to, 27 times. The first 10 amendments are called the Bill of Rights. These are the most important rights Americans have.

The Constitution and You

So, how does the Constitution work for you? The Constitution gives the U.S. government the power to make laws. Laws aren't just for adults. They're for kids, too.

There are laws that allow kids to go to school. Others say what kinds of jobs kids can have and how many hours they can work.

Amendment 1.

Congress shall make no law respecting an establishment of religion, or prohibiting the free exercise thereof; or abridging the freedom of speech, or of the press, or the right of it

Amendment 4.

The right of the people to be secure in their persons, houses, papers, and effects, against unreasonable searches and seizures, shall not be violated, and no Warrants shall issue, but upon probable cause, supported by Oath, or affirmation, and particularly describing the place to be searched,

You can see the original Constitution at the National Archives Building in Washington, D.C. The Bill of Rights and the Declaration of Independence are there, too.

21

For more than 200 years, the Constitution has kept the U.S. government strong. I'm proud of our Constitution. Now that you know its story, I hope you are, too!

The Framers of the Constitution

Some very patriotic men signed the Constitution. Many of them became important people in the history of the United States. Here are just a few:

George Washington was the president of the Constitutional Convention. He later became the first president of the United States. Today he is known as the Father of Our Country.

At 81 years old, *Benjamin Franklin* was the oldest signer of the Constitution. He helped make the country's first laws. He was also an inventor.

Alexander Hamilton favored a strong national government at the Constitutional Convention. He later worked on the U.S. banking system. He also became the Secretary of the Treasury.

James Madison kept records of what was said at the Constitutional Convention. He tried to help delegates work out their differences. That was how he became known as the Father of the Constitution. He later became the fourth president of the United States.

Glossary

amendment — an addition or correction

Congress — the group of people in the U.S. government who make laws

delegates — people who are chosen to speak for others

democracy — a kind of government in which the people make decisions by voting

Framers of the Constitution — the men who wrote the Constitution

national — belonging to a country

patriotic — showing love for one's own country

Revolutionary War — (1775–1783) the Colonies' fight for freedom from Great Britain; the Colonies later became the United States of America

symbol — an object that stands for something else

vote — to choose someone to work in the government

To Learn More

At the Library

Catrow, David. *We the Kids.*
New York: Dial Books for Young
Readers, 2002.

Hossell, Karen Price. *The Bill of Rights.*
Chicago: Heinemann Library, 2004.

Sobel, Syl. *The U.S. Constitution
and You.* Hauppauge, N.Y.: Barron's
Educational Series, 2001.

On the Web

To see a list of all 27 amendments,
visit *www.worldalmanacforkids.
com/explore/us_history/
constitution.html.*

FactHound offers a safe, fun way to
find Web sites related to this book. All
of the sites on FactHound have been
researched by our staff.

1. Visit *www.facthound.com*
2. Type in this special code:
   1404826432
3. Click on the FETCH IT button.

Your trusty FactHound will fetch the
best sites for you!

Index

Look for all of the books in the American Symbols series: